Waiting
FOR JESUS

THE FAMILY TREE OF JESUS & THE HOPE OF CHRISTMAS

THE DAILY GRACE CO.

Advent comes from the Latin word meaning "coming or arrival."

It is a season marked on the church calendar, beginning four Sundays before Christmas day. It is a season of waiting in which we look back to the days before Jesus's arrival and feel the longing that God's people had for the One to come. But as we are on this side of the cross, we are also in a state of longing – longing for Jesus to come again.

In *Waiting for Jesus: The Family Tree of Jesus and the Hope of Christmas*, we will be walking through Jesus's genealogy as given to us in the Gospel of Matthew. From Abraham to the birth of Jesus, we will trace the plan of God to send a savior, a deliverer, to save His people from their sins. We will see the neverending faithfulness of God on full display as He chooses to use common, sinful people in the lineage of His Son.

Each week begins with the lighting of Advent candles, accompanied by five days of devotions following various people in the lineage of Jesus. Family activities are included every week on the last day. You may want to consider looking ahead for planning purposes to ensure you have the needed supplies. Some weeks you may be busier than others, so use the activities as they work for your family.

We are praying that the Lord would be gracious to reveal Himself to you and your family as you walk through this devotional. May it bring you great delight in seeing His goodness and grace toward us in sending His Son, and may the eyes and hearts of our family members be opened to the good news of the gospel.

Merry Christmas!

Memory Verse

THIS HOPE WILL
NOT DISAPPOINT US,
BECAUSE GOD'S LOVE
HAS BEEN POURED
OUT IN OUR HEARTS
THROUGH THE HOLY
SPIRIT WHO WAS
GIVEN TO US.

ROMANS 5:5

WEEK 1 DAY 1

SCRIPTURE MEMORY & CANDLE LIGHTING DAY

Hope

The first candle of Advent represents
the hope that we have in Christ.

Prayer

God, You are our hope. You came to earth as a little baby, lived
a perfect life, and died on the cross for our sins. You promised
that whoever believes in You will be saved and live forever with
You in heaven. We know that You will keep Your word, and we
wait patiently for the day when we will see You face to face. This
Christmas, help us to want You more than presents. Help us to
pray, to know You better, and to place our hope in You.

We love You, Lord. Amen.

Waiting for Jesus

READ PSALM 27:14,
GALATIANS 4:4-5, MATTHEW 1:1

Have you ever had to wait a long time for something exciting? Maybe you waited for the rain to stop so you could go to the park. Maybe you waited for a birthday party. Maybe you waited until after dinner to eat a delicious bowl of ice cream. It can be really hard to be patient, but when we wait for something for a long time, it makes it so much better when we finally get to enjoy it. Waiting is not easy, but waiting can be good.

Christmas is an exciting day when we celebrate Jesus being born, but we have to wait for it. Today is the first day of a season called Advent. The word "advent" means "coming," and before Christmas we wait for the coming of Jesus.

God promised to send His Son, Jesus, a long, long time ago. When God made the first people, they lived with God in the garden of Eden. Everything was wonderful, but Adam and Eve disobeyed God. They sinned. God warned them that if they disobeyed Him, they would die. But God loved His people so much that He promised to send someone to save them. He promised to give an offspring—a child—who would make everything right and give God's people eternal life. We all sin, so we deserve to die too. But God sent Jesus, His perfect Son, to die in our place so that we can live forever with God if we believe in Him.

It took a long time for Jesus to come, and it was not always easy to be patient, but God was working through Jesus's family tree—his grandparents, great-grandparents, and great-great-grandparents—to bring Jesus at the perfect time.

God used regular people in Jesus's family tree to make His big promise come true. During Advent, we wait for Christmas just like God's people waited for Jesus to be born, but we are also waiting for Him to come again! One day, Jesus is going to come back, and all of the sad and hard things will be over. Waiting can be hard, but our joy will be even greater!

DISCUSS TOGETHER

IF YOU HAVE EVER HAD TO WAIT A LONG TIME FOR SOMETHING, WHAT WAS IT? WHAT WAS IT LIKE WHEN YOU FINALLY GOT TO EXPERIENCE IT?

WHY ARE YOU EXCITED TO CELEBRATE JESUS BEING BORN? WHY ARE YOU EXCITED FOR HIM TO COME AGAIN?

Prayer

Father God, thank You for sending Jesus to save us from our sins. Even though we deserve to die because we disobey, You loved us so much that You gave Your perfect Son to die for us. God, we are often impatient, please help us to trust You while we wait for You to fulfill your promises to us. Teach us to want You more than anything else, and help us to long for Christ this Advent season. Amen.

Draw a picture

about what you learned today.

Abraham

READ GENESIS 12:1-2, 7

Everybody has a family tree. A family tree is a chart showing members of your family. Your grandparents are in your family tree, and so are your great-grandparents and your great-great-grandparents. Another name for a family tree is a genealogy. The gospel of Matthew starts with the genealogy of Jesus, and it shows how God worked through a family to bring the promised Savior.

The first name in Jesus's genealogy in Matthew is Abraham. God chose to use Abraham in a very special way to bring us Jesus but not because of anything Abraham did. In fact, Abraham didn't seem like a very good choice at all. Abraham was a sinner. He did not worship God, but God chose him anyway.

God made big promises to Abraham and his wife, Sarah. They didn't have any kids, but God promised to give them more kids, grandkids, and great-grandkids than they could count! God also promised to give Abraham and his offspring a wonderful land where they could live with God forever. God promised to make Abraham's offspring a blessing to people from every nation in the world! Abraham believed God would keep all His promises, and Abraham believed God would send Jesus.

Abraham and Sarah saw some of God's promises, but the world would have to wait a long time for God to answer them all. That's because Jesus, the offspring of Abraham, would be the answer to God's promises. When we believe in Jesus like Abraham did, we become Abraham's children, and we have the blessing of eternal life that God promised to Abraham. When Jesus comes back, He is going to bring that perfect land where everyone who believes in Him will live forever.

DISCUSS TOGETHER

ABRAHAM SINNED AGAINST GOD, BUT GOD STILL CHOSE TO BLESS HIM. HAVE YOU EVER DONE SOMETHING WRONG?

DO YOU BELIEVE THAT GOD WILL KEEP HIS PROMISES?

Prayer

Dear God, thank You for sending Jesus even though we sin against You. Thank You for choosing to bless people like Abraham and like us. We know that we cannot do anything to earn Your love, and we praise You for your grace to us. Thank You for making a promise to Abraham and for letting us be a part of Abraham's family and blessing if we trust in Jesus. Amen.

Draw a pitcure

about what you learned today.

Isaac

READ GENESIS 17:15-22

God made a promise to Abraham that He would never break.
This promise is called a covenant. Part of this covenant was
that Abraham would have lots of kids. God told Abraham that
he would have as many kids as stars in the sky! Best of all,
somewhere in Abraham's family line would be Jesus, the
promised Redeemer!

But there was a problem: Abraham and Sarah could not have
kids. Up until that point, Sarah's body could not grow a baby,
But that didn't stop God. God knew that He was the only one
who could fulfill this promise. Abraham knew it too, and he
had faith in God to keep His promise.

More than twenty years later, Sarah still did not have a baby.
Abraham and Sarah were getting old and sometimes doubted
God, but God did not change His plan or His promise. He told
Abraham that Sarah would have a baby the next year and to
name the baby Isaac (Genesis 17:19). And guess what? Everything
happened exactly as God said it would! Sarah had baby Isaac
when she was 90, and Abraham was 100 years old. Isaac was a
miracle, and God chose to pass on His promise through Isaac.

The story of Isaac reminds us of another miraculous birth – the
birth of Jesus. Just as Abraham and Sarah waited a long time
for Isaac, God's people waited and waited for Jesus to be born.
Jesus came, just as God said He would, down the family line of
Abraham and Isaac! We can trust that God will also fulfill His
promise to come again. We can wait with confidence because
God always keeps His promises.

SOMETIMES PEOPLE MAKE PROMISES THEY CANNOT KEEP. HAVE YOU EVER MADE A PROMISE THAT YOU KNEW YOU COULD NOT KEEP?

GOD NEVER MAKES PROMISES HE CANNOT KEEP. IN THE STORY OF ISAAC, HOW DID GOD SHOW US HE IS A PROMISE KEEPER? HOW DOES THIS STORY OF ISAAC ENCOURAGE YOU TO TRUST GOD?

Prayer

Dear God, thank You for always keeping Your promises, even when it looks impossible. Nothing is impossible for You. You have shown us again and again in the Bible that we can trust You. You sent Isaac like You said You would. You sent Jesus like You said You would. So in our waiting, we can trust You. You will come again to make Your kingdom new because You said You would. Amen.

Draw a pitcure

about what you learned today.

Jacob

READ GENESIS 28:10-17

Do you ever feel like you aren't as good as other people who follow Jesus? We might think the people in the Bible were amazing, but if we look closely at the stories of the people in Jesus's family tree, we will find lots of people who struggled to believe and obey God. God loved and used them anyway. Jacob was one of those people.

Jacob was Isaac's son and Abraham's grandson. He was a sneaky man who sometimes lied to get his way. He tricked his brother, Esau, and took something that did not belong to him. He even dressed up as his brother to trick their blind dad into giving him an important family blessing. But God still had plans for Jacob. He appeared to Jacob in a dream, standing at the top of a tall ladder that went all the way to heaven. God promised to bless the whole world through Jacob's family. Does that remind you of God's promise to Abraham? It should! God was keeping His promise to Abraham through Jacob. He gave Jacob twelve sons, and many years later, Jesus was born from one of those families. Jesus lived a perfect life, died on the cross for our sins, and rose again from the dead. That is the blessing God promised to Jacob, and it is the promise we get to enjoy when we repent of our sins and believe in Jesus.

Jacob might have been a sinful man, but God sent our sinless Savior through Jacob's family to fix our sin problem. If we believe in Jesus, we will be saved and live forever with God. Jesus came for the Jacobs of the world like you and me. He is the ladder in Jacob's dream that brings us back to God.

DISCUSS TOGETHER

LIKE JACOB, HAVE YOU EVER LIED TO SOMEONE OR TRICKED SOMEONE TO GET WHAT YOU WANTED?

EVEN THOUGH JACOB MADE MANY MISTAKES, GOD STILL USED HIM. HOW DO YOU THINK GOD COULD USE YOU?

Prayer

Dear Lord, we thank You for using regular people like us to grow Your kingdom. Thank You for blessing us with a Savior from Jacob's family who was born in Bethlehem, lived a perfect life, and died on the cross to pay for our sins. Help us to share the good news of Jesus with others so that more people can be a part of Your family. Amen.

Draw a picture
about what you learned today.

Judah

READ GENESIS 49:8-12, REVELATION 5:5

Jacob had twelve sons, but his favorite son was Joseph. So why would we look at Judah? Well, even though Jacob did not choose Judah, God did. God chose Judah to be the one through whom Jesus would come!

Just as we have seen with others in Jesus's family tree, Judah was not perfect. Remember the favored son, Joseph, we were talking about? The brothers did not like that Joseph was their dad's favorite. Judah and his brothers wanted to get rid of him, so they sold him to some traveling Ishmaelites. Judah was the one who wanted to sell his brother so that he could get money for himself. But that was not the only thing Judah did wrong. He sinned against his son's wife, and even though she did things that did not honor God, his sin against her was even worse.

But God used Judah's failures to grow him. That is what God does! When Judah was older, he offered to give himself in exchange for one of his brothers. That sacrifice points forward to the sacrifice of Christ and the way He gave His life in exchange for us. Before Jacob died, he gave a blessing to Judah that pointed forward to Jesus coming. Jesus would come, and He will come again to rule as King forever. We would not expect Jesus, a king, to be born from people who made terrible mistakes, but Judah's story shows us that God uses broken, sinful people to fulfill His big promises.

WHY DO YOU THINK GOD CHOSE THE LINE OF JUDAH
TO BE THE LINEAGE OF JESUS?

HAVE YOU EVER THOUGHT THAT YOUR SIN AND
MISTAKES WILL MAKE YOU UNABLE TO BE USED BY GOD?
HOW CAN YOU HAVE HOPE THAT GOD USES EVEN OUR
FAULTS TO ACCOMPLISH HIS PURPOSES?

Prayer

God, thank You for choosing the unchosen, the
unfavored, and deeply sinful people to accomplish
Your purposes. Thank You for the promise of royalty
in the blessing of Judah. Thank You that through
Judah, You would send Your son, Jesus, to be the
Savior of the world. May we rejoice that Jesus was
Your plan all along! May this season turn our hearts
to celebrate the fact that Jesus has come and that He
will come again as the Lion of Judah! Amen.

Draw a picture

about what you learned today.

REFLECTION & FAMILY ACTIVITY

Make Your Own Family Tree

This week, you were introduced to Jesus's family tree, or genealogy. Just like Jesus, we all have a family tree too, even though it is likely we cannot trace ours back quite as far. To help us understand what a family tree looks like, we are going to create a family tree of our own! This visual will help us as we continue learning about the genealogy of Christ over the next several weeks.

INSTRUCTIONS

1. Using note cards or paper cut into a similar size, begin by writing your name and the names of any brothers and sisters, each on a separate card. These cards will form the base, or bottom, of your family tree.

2. Next, create cards for your parents, grandparents, great-grandparents. If you have enough time, you can also include any aunts, uncles, and cousins. These cards will form the top layers of the tree.

3. Noting someone's heritage can help us understand more about a family. Once you have made sure there is a card for each person who is part of your family tree, using stickers or simply drawing pictures or writing short sentences, add to each card everything you know about that person. You might include where they were born and where they grew up, how long they lived, their personalities, things they liked or enjoyed – anything you know that comes to mind!

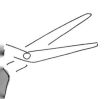

4. The last step is to find a place in your home – an empty wall space, the back of a bedroom door, or a larger piece of paper to be used as a temporary poster – and using tape, place the cards in layers, each generation forming a new layer, or row, above the last.

here's an example!

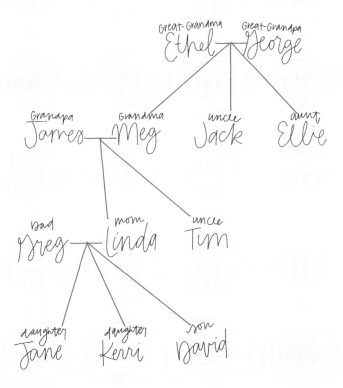

Great-Grandma
Ethel

Great-Grandpa
George

Grandpa
James

Grandma
Meg

uncle
Jack

aunt
Ellie

Dad
Greg

mom
Linda

uncle
Tim

daughter
Jane

daughter
Kerri

son
David

Memory Verse

FOR A CHILD WILL BE BORN FOR US, A SON WILL BE GIVEN TO US, AND THE GOVERNMENT WILL BE ON HIS SHOULDERS. HE WILL BE NAMED WONDERFUL COUNSELOR, MIGHTY GOD, ETERNAL FATHER, PRINCE OF PEACE.

ISAIAH 9:6

SCRIPTURE MEMORY AND CANDLE LIGHTING

Peace

The second candle represents the peace offered
to us through Christ.

Prayer

God, You are our peace. Even when we feel overwhelmed
or scared, You are always with us.

Jesus, because You came and lived a perfect life and died the
death we deserved, You made a way for us to have peace with
God. God, would You help me trust You more? Would You
bring peace to my family this Christmas season? Would You
bring rest when I am tired and calmness when I am stressed?
Thank You Jesus for all You did for us. We love You.

Amen.

READ GENESIS 38:6-14, 24-30

Note to parents: There are difficult topics presented in today's reading. You may want to read this story prior to discussing with your children, deciding how to wisely discuss certain elements, depending on age appropriation and your own comfort level of addressing topics presented.

The family of Jesus was not perfect. It was filled with people and stories that are sad, messy, and difficult. Tamar is one of those stories. She was a woman married to a man named Er and welcomed into the family of Judah. Er was disobedient and did not fulfill his duties as a husband to her, so he died, and Tamar became a widow. It was custom at that time for the brother-in-law to marry the widow so they could have children and keep the family name. So, Er's brother, Onan, married Tamar. But Onan was selfish and did not want to carry on the name of his brother to his children, so he was disobedient and lost his life too. Tamar was left widowed again and without children. She was sad, alone, and did not know what to do! Her father-in-law, Judah, was afraid of giving her another son to marry, and he sent her away with an empty promise of finding her when his youngest son could marry.

But time passed, and Judah never kept his promise. His promise was a lie, and he continued in disobedience just like his sons. Tamar was likely angry and came up with a plan to trick Judah into giving her a child because he would not provide her a son to marry. Though her plan was wicked, it worked, and she was able to trick Judah into giving her twins. At first, Judah was outraged and wanted Tamar to die! But then God changed His heart, and he realized that her actions were provoked by the sins of his sons and his own sin, too. Judah repented to God and spared Tamar's life.

This story might leave us scratching our heads, but it teaches us something about God that is important. It teaches us that God can use all kinds of people to accomplish His plan. It teaches us that even if we mess up, God never messes up, and He will do everything He says He will do! Though Tamar's family was messy, God promised to use them in the family tree to one day bring His perfect Son, Jesus Christ, into the world to save sinners. Because God keeps His promises even when we do not, Jesus came and offers salvation to sinners who repent and believe in Him as their Savior.

DISCUSS TOGETHER

IN THIS STORY, SIN LEADS TO MORE SIN. OUR SIN DOES NOT JUST AFFECT US; IT CAN AFFECT OTHERS AROUND US TOO. HOW DO WE SEE EVIDENCE OF THIS IN THE LIFE OF JUDAH, HIS SONS, AND TAMAR? WHO LEADS THEM TO REPENT OF THEIR SIN?

HAVE YOU EVER MADE A PROMISE THAT YOU DID NOT KEEP? HOW DOES THIS STORY SHOW US THAT GOD ALWAYS KEEPS HIS PROMISES EVEN WHEN WE DO NOT?

Prayer

Dear Lord, we are so thankful that You keep your promises to us. We are reminded of the promise of redemption You offer us through the gift of Your one and only Son, Jesus Christ, who You sent to save sinners who repent and put their faith in Him. Thank You for welcoming every kind of person to receive that gift—even sinners like us. We pray we would cling to this promise and trust in Your unfailing plans for us. Amen.

Draw a pitcure
about what you learned today.

Rahab

READ JOSHUA 2:1-21, JOSHUA 6:22-25

There are only five women named in Jesus's family tree. One of these women had a bad reputation before God changed her life. Her name was Rahab, and she lived in Jericho. Jericho was a city with huge walls around it. It was in the land God promised to give His people. Jericho was full of people who did not worship God and did not like His people. Rahab's home was in one of the walls of the city, and it was a place where lots of people stopped for information about Jericho and to spend time with Rahab in ways that did not honor God.* However, Rahab knew all the things God did to deliver Israel from Egypt and other enemies, so she believed He must be the one true God.

When Israel sent two spies into Jericho to see if they could conquer the city, the spies stayed at Rahab's house. Because she was more afraid of God than the men of Jericho, Rahab hid the spies from the king and kept them safe. She asked them to protect her family when they came back. With a rope, she lowered them out the window of her home. They told her to hang a red rope out of her window so that they would know which house to protect when they came back. When the spies returned with all of Israel to conquer the city, they remembered Rahab, saw the red rope in her window, and protected her family.

Later, Rahab married an Israelite named Salmon from the tribe of Judah. She had a son named Boaz, and her great-great-grandson was King David. From her family came Jesus, the one God promised to send to bless everyone on earth. He did not just come for the people of Israel but for anyone who would believe in Him and turn away from sin. The story of Rahab shows us that God can change our lives completely. No matter where we grow up or what mistakes we've made, when we believe in Jesus, He makes us new. He rescues us from sin and makes us part of God's family.

DISCUSS TOGETHER

WHY DID RAHAB HIDE THE SPIES FROM THE KING AND THE PEOPLE OF JERICHO?

WHEN WE BELIEVE IN JESUS, OUR LIVES ARE CHANGED. READ GALATIANS 2:20, AND DISCUSS HOW OUR LIVES ARE CHANGED IN CHRIST.

Prayer

Dear Lord, we are so thankful that You desire people from all kinds of backgrounds to be part of Your family. Thank You for including us! Thank You for sending Jesus as a baby who grew up to pay for our sins so that we can become new creatures when we believe in Him. Help us to fear You more than we fear men and to obey You with all of our hearts. Amen.

Draw a picture

about what you learned today.

Parents, if you have older children, consider talking to them about Rahab's profession as a prostitute in light of the New Testament references to her faith (see Hebrews 11:31 and James 2:25). What does her inclusion in Jesus's family teach us about our sin and God's grace?

Ruth

READ RUTH 1:16-17, RUTH 2:11-12

God knew what He was doing when He made His family tree. The next person, Ruth, was a Gentile, which means she was not from one of the tribes of Israel. She was from Moab, which was a big deal because Moabites were enemies of Israel. But God still included Ruth in the royal family tree.

Ruth had many hard things happen in her life. Her husband died, and she had no children. Her husband's mother, Naomi, told her to go back to her own family to find a new husband. But instead, Ruth went back to Bethlehem with Naomi. She was loyal to Naomi and trusted God. So she left her country and started working in the fields of Bethlehem so that she and Naomi would have food to eat.

Ruth was working in the field of Boaz, a rich and godly man who would be the family's kinsman-redeemer. This was a part of Israel's law that said an unmarried man should marry a widow within the family to provide for her and give her a son to carry on the family name. Boaz married Ruth, and God gave them a son named Obed. Obed was the grandfather of King David, and this is the line through which King Jesus comes!

The story of Ruth teaches us that God's grace is for all kinds of people. Ruth trusted God, and God brought her into His family and took care of her. Boaz gives us a picture of Jesus. Just as Boaz was able and willing to save Ruth and her family, Jesus is the only one who is able to save us, and He willingly does so! No matter what we are going through, we can put our faith in Jesus and become part of God's family.

THE REASON FOR CHRISTMAS IS JESUS. IN JESUS,
WE ARE NO LONGER ENEMIES OF GOD BUT
CHILDREN OF GOD! HOW DOES THE STORY OF
RUTH SHOW US THIS TRUTH?

THE STORY OF RUTH TELLS US THE GOSPEL.
THE GOSPEL IS THE GOOD NEWS THAT JESUS
CAME TO SAVE PEOPLE FROM THEIR SINS.
IT DOES NOT MATTER WHO YOU ARE OR WHAT
YOU HAVE DONE. SALVATION IS A FREE GIFT
OF GRACE TO ALL WHO PUT THEIR FAITH IN
JESUS. HAVE YOU PUT YOUR FAITH IN JESUS?

Prayer

Dear God, thank You for including all sorts of people
in Your family. Thank You for showing us this in the
story of Ruth. Thank You for Jesus. Not only was He the
only one able to save us, but He was willing to. He came
as a baby, lived a sinless life, died on the cross for our
sins, and rose again. We can receive the gift of salvation
by putting our faith in You. What grace this is! Thank
You! In Jesus's name we pray, Amen.

Draw a picture
about what you learned today.

Jesse

READ 1 SAMUEL 16:10-13, ISAIAH 11:1-16,
MATTHEW 1:5-6

There are people in the Old Testament called prophets. God used prophets to send messages to His people. These messages were called prophecies and were used to give warnings and promises for the future. God used the prophet Isaiah to tell God's people that Jesus would be born into the family of a man named Jesse. God's people were very happy to hear this promise. They were living in a time when their kings were not following God, and they were hoping for a good king to make things right.

Jesse of Bethlehem was an ordinary shepherd with eight sons. His youngest son, David, watched over sheep for him. One day another prophet, Samuel, came to Jesse's house and met with David. While he was there, Samuel said that God chose David to be the king, and years later, he did become king! David was not the true and perfect King, but he pointed to the true King, Jesus.

Jesus's family tree branched out from Jesse to David and his children. At the time of Jesus's birth, everyone from David's family had to return to the town of Bethlehem because a census was being taken. Since Joseph and Mary were part of David's family, they traveled from Nazareth to Bethlehem. In Bethlehem, Jesus Christ, the perfect King and promised Savior of the world, was born.

DISCUSS TOGETHER

WHAT IS A PROPHECY? WHO DOES ISAIAH PROPHESY
WILL COME FROM THE FAMILY OF JESSE?
DOES THAT PROPHECY COME TRUE?

JESSE WAS JESUS'S 26TH GREAT-GRANDFATHER IN
HIS FAMILY TREE. THAT IS A LOT OF "GREATS"!
SEE HOW MANY PEOPLE YOU CAN NAME
IN YOUR OWN FAMILY TREE.

Prayer

Dear Lord, we praise You for loving and caring for us
in so many ways and even bringing us into this world!
We thank You for the gift of family. We thank You for
placing us intentionally in the family we are in. We thank
You for preserving generations of families so that Jesus
Christ could fulfill the promise of the prophets as the true
and perfect Savior and King. Remind us that You have a
special purpose and plan for our lives. Everything You
have given us is meant to be used to the glory of Your
name and the furthering of Your kingdom! Help us to
honor You in everything that we do. Amen.

Draw a picture

about what you learned today.

David

READ I SAMUEL 16:1-13, 2 SAMUEL 7:8-17,
LUKE 1:30-33

David was a shepherd and the youngest boy in his family. One day while he was with his sheep in the field, God called David and chose him to become king over all of Israel. Throughout his life, David was used by God in mighty ways. He defeated the giant, Goliath, and other enemies of Israel. He loved God with all his heart and was called a man after God's own heart. But David also sinned. He disobeyed God many times.

Even though David sinned, God still put David in Jesus's family tree. God did not choose David because he was perfect; He chose him because He loved him. God made David a promise that He would build him a house and give his offspring a kingdom that would last forever. The answer to this very big promise would be Jesus! Many years later, one of David's descendents was born in Bethlehem, and his name was Jesus. David was a shepherd who took care of sheep, but Jesus is the Good Shepherd who takes care of God's children. David was king over Israel for a little while, but Jesus will be King of the whole universe forever and ever! David was not a perfect king, but Jesus is.

DISCUSS TOGETHER

DAVID SINNED BUT SAID, "I'M SORRY," AND GOD FORGAVE HIM. HAVE YOU EVER ASKED GOD TO FORGIVE YOU OF YOUR SINS?

OPTIONAL: AS A FAMILY, READ PSALM 51, AND TALK ABOUT CONFESSION AND FORGIVENESS.

HOW ARE DAVID AND JESUS SIMILAR? IN WHAT WAYS IS JESUS THE PERFECT VERSION OF DAVID?

Prayer

Lord, thank You for Your promises. No one is perfect except You, and You freely offer forgiveness to all who ask. Thank You, Lord. Thank You, Jesus, for coming as a baby to redeem this broken world. You are the Good Shepherd who leads and guides us each day. Just as David looked forward to Your coming, so we await Your return. Come and make all things new, we pray. Amen.

Draw a picture

about what you learned today.

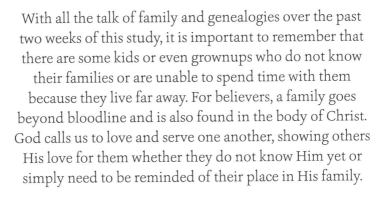

REFLECTION & FAMILY ACTIVITY

Bake a Sweet Treat for Your Neighbor

With all the talk of family and genealogies over the past two weeks of this study, it is important to remember that there are some kids or even grownups who do not know their families or are unable to spend time with them because they live far away. For believers, a family goes beyond bloodline and is also found in the body of Christ. God calls us to love and serve one another, showing others His love for them whether they do not know Him yet or simply need to be reminded of their place in His family.

Jesus came to earth to die so that we could be adopted into His family as sons and daughters. That is how much He loves us. When we have opportunities, we want to show others that love, and we can do that often through even the smallest acts of kindness.

INSTRUCTIONS

For this week's activity, take some time to bake a sweet treat to share. This can be as simple as break n' bake cookies or boxed brownies or as fancy as mixing your own cookie dough from scratch (see recipe attached!), using fun cookie cutters, and decorating with Christmas sprinkles and icing. Place the finished

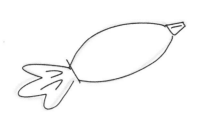

treats in a bag, plastic container, or on a covered plate, adding a short note with a Bible verse. Take them to someone you know who might be lonely this season. This could be a neighbor on your street, someone you know from church, or a friend you know from school.

Sugar Cookies

BAKE: 400° FOR 8-10 MINUTES   **YIELDS:** 6 DOZEN COOKIES

CREAM TOGETHER:

1 c. powdered sugar
1 c. butter, softened
1 c. granulated sugar

ADD:

2 eggs, beaten
1 c. vegetable oil
2 tsp. vanilla
1 tsp. baking powder
¼ tsp. salt
5 c. flour
1 tsp. cream of tartar

INSTRUCTIONS:

Roll into small balls. Place on ungreased baking sheet. Press each cookie gently using the bottom of a small glass dipped in sugar or a decorative cookie stamp. Bake as directed above.

Memory Verse

BUT THE ANGEL SAID
TO THEM, "DON'T BE
AFRAID, FOR LOOK,
I PROCLAIM TO YOU
GOOD NEWS OF GREAT
JOY THAT WILL BE
FOR ALL THE PEOPLE:
TODAY IN THE CITY OF
DAVID A SAVIOR WAS
BORN FOR YOU,
WHO IS THE MESSIAH,
THE LORD.

LUKE 2:10-11

SCRIPTURE MEMORY AND CANDLE LIGHTING

Joy

The third candle represents the joy found in Christ.

Prayer

God, You make us happy. You are better than all the cookies, ornaments, and presents we could ask for this Christmas. Just as the shepherds rejoiced that dark night when the angels appeared, so we are so happy that You came to earth! You lived just like us – eating, sleeping, and obeying your mom, except you did it all perfectly. Because You came and died on the cross, You made a way for our sins to be forgiven, and You set us free! You are all we need, Jesus. Amen.

Uriah, Bathsheba, and Solomon

READ 2 SAMUEL 11 AND 12

David was God's anointed king. He was a good king, but he did not always choose to obey God. One day, David chose to break God's law. A man named Uriah was one of David's most trusted military officers. While Uriah was away fighting at war, David saw Uriah's wife, Bathsheba, and decided to steal her for himself and commit adultery. Bathsheba became pregnant, and David tried to cover up his sin by having Uriah killed. God saw what David did and was angry. But what God did next is surprising! He sent a prophet named Nathan to confront David so that he would repent of his sin. By God's mercy, David realized his sin and asked for the Lord's forgiveness. Though there were consequences for David, God forgave him and later blessed him.

Even in this sad story, God brought about good. No matter how many times we mess up, God has a plan, and He will bring it to be! Just as He made a plan to bring Jesus into the world through David's family, God still remained faithful to His promise when David disobeyed. God gave David and Bathsheba a son named Solomon. Through him, the lineage leading up to the Messiah lived on. Even with lots of bad choices, God made good things happen. Through this story, we are reminded that even when we are unfaithful, God is faithful, and we can trust that He fulfills every promise He ever makes—just like the promise of our Savior, Jesus Christ.

WHEN WAS A TIME YOU SINNED AND
TRIED TO COVER IT UP?

READ 1 JOHN 1:9. WHAT DOES GOD DO
WHEN WE REPENT? WHY IS REPENTANCE BETTER
THAN TRYING TO HIDE SIN?

Prayer

Thank You, Lord, for Your faithfulness to us even
when we are unfaithful. You delight in repentance, and
we pray we would be a family quick to confess our sin
and run to You for forgiveness. We thank You for Your
grace in working through our lives even when we mess
up or get in the way. And we thank You for working
through every single moment in time to bring us a
Savior to save us from our sin. Amen.

Draw a pitcure
about what you learned today.

The Line of Kings

READ MATTHEW 1:7-10

After Solomon died, his son, Rehoboam, became king. He was a bad king. He did not listen to the wise men who had instructed his father. A few years after he became king, the nation of Israel, who was united when David was king, was divided into two – the northern kingdom of Israel and the southern kingdom of Judah.

In Matthew 1:7-10, there are names of kings in the line that came after Rehoboam, but some of the names were left out. And guess what? Most of those guys were bad too. Some kings were good but then started making bad decisions. It was a hopeless cycle. Even when there was the occasional good king, it would not be long before a king would come after him who was wicked again.

Israel wanted a king but not this kind of king. They wanted a king who would do good for the people and rule in righteousness, peace, and love. But this kind of king would be hard to find since every king had the same sin problem all of us have. Some would rule wickedly. Some would treat others unjustly. Some would use their power to hurt others. All of these bad kings made the people wish for a better king – a king who would come and rule justly. God would send Jesus to be this true King. During advent, we wait for King Jesus to be born just like the people of Israel did.

DO YOU THINK YOU WOULD BE A GOOD KING?
WHY OR WHY NOT?

WHY IS JESUS THE BETTER KING?

Prayer

God, we are saddened to look at the history of Israel and see how the kings ruled in wickedness. They hurt people You loved and did what was evil in Your eyes. God, we know that we too are guilty of doing evil in Your eyes. We hurt people You love. Forgive us for our sin. God, thank You that we do not have to hope in worldly kings or in ourselves, for You are our perfect King. You love perfectly, rule righteously, and will never do wrong. Help us to trust in You. Amen.

Draw a pitcure

about what you learned today.

Josiah

READ 2 CHRONICLES 34:1-7, 2 CHRONICLES 34:14-28

Josiah became king when he was only 8 years old! Can you imagine being a king at that age? Josiah did not use his royal authority for selfish purposes but instead looked to God and helped the people worship Him. Josiah got rid of fake gods and told the people to rebuild the temple, which had been destroyed. One day, while men were working on the temple, they found the Word of God, which had been lost. While Josiah read it, he cried because he realized that the people had disobeyed God for a long time. He knew that they deserved to be punished. But even though judgment would come, God promised there would be peace during Josiah's life because he sought the Lord.

Josiah did not always obey the Lord. One day, God told Josiah not to go to battle, but he went anyway, wearing a disguise. He was shot in battle and died that day. Even though Josiah was a godly king, he was not perfect. His life pointed to the need for a better king—one who would obey God perfectly.

And guess what? That king was coming. Jesus was the perfect King who led His people with wisdom and love. He always obeyed God, even when it cost Him His life. He lived a perfect life and died for the sins of not only Josiah but all who would trust in Him. He promised that whoever repents of their sin and trusts in Him will find eternal life. We are never too young to follow the Lord. Just as Josiah trusted in God when he was still a kid, Jesus invites all to come to him, whether young or old. Have you trusted in Jesus as your King?

DISCUSS TOGETHER

WHAT WOULD YOU DO IF YOU WERE KING OR QUEEN FOR A DAY?

JOSIAH SOUGHT TO OBEY THE LORD AS A KID, EVEN WHEN HIS PARENTS DID NOT. HOW DOES THIS ENCOURAGE YOU TO TRUST GOD NO MATTER WHAT?

Prayer

Lord, You are the perfect King. Just as Josiah sinned against You, so do we. Thank You Jesus for coming to earth as a little baby and for being the perfect King and ruler. You did what we could not and sacrificed Yourself so that we could be saved. Thank You, Lord! Help us to know Your Word better and learn more about You. Help us to follow You and desire to obey You, no matter what others around us choose to do. Jesus, thank You for being the perfect one who came to set us free. Amen.

Draw a pitcure
about what you learned today.

Exile and Deportation to Babylon

READ 2 KINGS 24-25:21, JEREMIAH 33:6-16

When people are exiled, they are forced to leave their home or country. Can you imagine how sad that would be? Exile even happened to God's people. The kingdom of Judah was supposed to be a holy nation who glorified God. They were supposed to show their love for God by worshiping Him and obeying His law, but four bad kings ruled in Judah after King Josiah. These kings did not worship God and were very cruel. Because of their bad leadership, the people of Judah disobeyed God. God loved His people and did not want them to be destroyed by their sin, so he was patient and gave them time to ask for forgiveness. But, the people of Judah wanted to keep on sinning.

As a result of their sin, enemies could easily attack the kingdom of Judah, and they fell to Babylon. King Nebuchadnezzar of Babylon captured the people of Judah and destroyed their land. The people were very sad and cried for God to save them. They were lost and alone in exile, away from their home, but God sent the prophet Jeremiah to speak comfort and hope to them. God promised to bring them back home and to bring a good king who would obey God and help them love God.

Jesus is this good King, and He helps us follow God. Sin separated us from God, but Jesus brings us back. When we believe in Him, He forgives us for all the ways we disobeyed. This world is not our home, but when Jesus comes back again, He will bring us to our forever home in heaven with God where peace will last forever.

HOW DO YOU FEEL WHEN YOU ARE AWAY FROM HOME?

HOW DOES IT FEEL TO KNOW THAT THERE
IS PEACE AND SAFETY IN GOD'S PRESENCE
THROUGH JESUS?

Prayer

Dear Father, You are the true God who sees our lonely hearts. You comfort and let us know that through Jesus we always have a home in Your presence. If we cling to Jesus, Your love will hold us secure and will not exile us. We thank You that King Jesus was birthed into the world to bring us back to You. We confess that at times, we wander from Your Word. But we ask that this Advent season, we remember the first coming of Jesus and Your mission to restore the lost. Help our hearts to remain in You and to await Jesus's second coming when He will finally bring us to our heavenly home. Amen.

Draw a picture
about what you learned today.

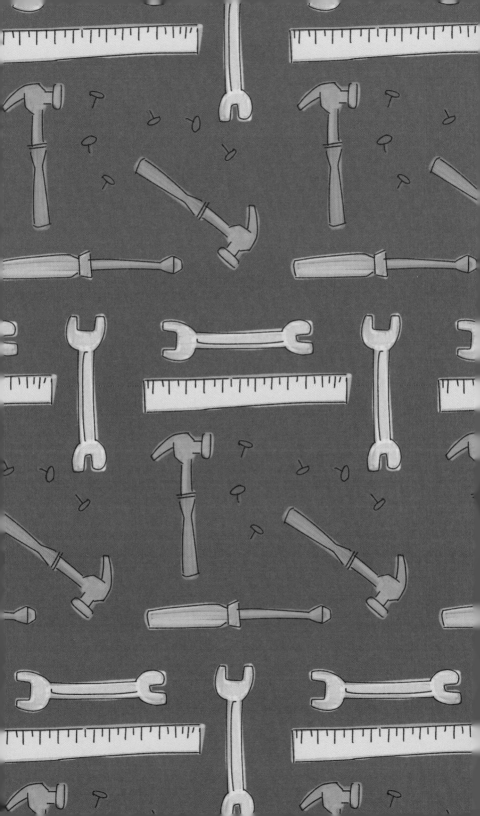

Return to Jerusalem

READ EZRA 3:7-4:5, HAGGAI 2:20-23

The temple was the place where God lived, and His presence gave His people hope. When the Babylonians captured the kingdom of Judah, they destroyed the temple. God's people were sent away, and they wanted to come home and rebuild the temple. God's people had been captured and were ruled by the king of Persia, but God softened his heart. God's people missed their home, and king Cyrus of Persia felt sad for them and let them go back to rebuild God's house.

A man named Zerubbabel helped the people build the foundation for the temple. Some people were excited, but some people were sad because it wasn't as good as the last temple. When some enemies came and started trouble, God's people stopped building the new temple. They were discouraged and went back to their own homes and forgot about God's mission to rebuild Jerusalem.

But God sent a prophet named Haggai to tell them to obey God and keep building! God promised that He would get rid of all the bad kings and bring a better kingdom. The people were building a temple now, but one day God would give a better temple. Jesus said that He was the true temple. He is God who became a man to live with us. During Advent we can celebrate that Jesus is "God with us," and one day He will come again, and the presence of God will be with us forever.

JESUS IS "GOD WITH US." WHY DO WE CELEBRATE THAT JESUS CAME TO LIVE ON EARTH?

ONE DAY JESUS WILL COME AGAIN, AND GOD WILL LIVE WITH US. WHAT DO YOU THINK THAT WILL BE LIKE?

Prayer

Dear Father, You are the Light of the World. No one can make it through this life unless You light the path. Thank You for showing us the way to Jesus who has conquered the darkness of sin. Thank You that Jesus is the true temple who radiates Your glory and reveals You to us. We are so grateful that through Jesus, Your presence is always near. Your Spirit is in us, making us Your living temples to restore Your creation. Lord, we confess that at times, we do not care for the temple of our bodies. We live in ways that do not please You. So, we ask that You would help us be more like Jesus who was the perfect temple. And, keep our eyes on heaven, looking for Jesus's return and the coming of Your eternal temple. Amen.

Draw a pitcure

about what you learned today.

REFLECTION & FAMILY ACTIVITY

Enjoy a Family Candlelight Dinner with Christmas Music

On Day 1 of this week, we lit a candle to represent the joy found in Christ. Our Advent ornament for the same day was a sun to represent Jesus being the source of our true joy. This activity is a reminder of that—in the darkness of this world and in anything we may go through, He is our light. Jesus came and lit up a dark world filled with sin, and He calls us to carry that light to others so that they may know Him too.

Tonight, enjoy a family candlelight dinner. If you do not have extra candles around your home, you can use your advent candles. Pick out some of your favorite Christmas hymns or carols too, and play them in the background, or take some time to sing a carol together before or after dinner. Focus your conversation by going around the table and letting each family member share one or two ways that Christ is our true joy this season and throughout the rest of the year.

Joy to the World

Joy to the world! the Lord is come; Let

earth re - ceive her King; Let

ev - 'ry heart pre - pare Him room, And

heav'n and na - ture sing, And heav'n and na - ture sing, And

And heav'n and na - ture sing, And heav'n and na - ture

heav'n,__ and heav'n and na - ture sing.

sing,

FOR GOD LOVED THE
WORLD IN THIS WAY:
HE GAVE HIS ONE
AND ONLY SON, SO
THAT EVERYONE WHO
BELIEVES IN HIM WILL
NOT PERISH BUT HAVE
ETERNAL LIFE. FOR GOD
DID NOT SEND HIS SON
INTO THE WORLD TO
CONDEMN THE WORLD,
BUT TO SAVE THE
WORLD THROUGH HIM.

JOHN 3:16-17

SCRIPTURE MEMORY AND CANDLE LIGHTING

Love

The final Advent candle represents God's love.

Prayer

God, thank You for Your love. You loved us so much that You left the beauty of heaven and came down to earth as a little baby. You love us completely. When You came, You were hungry, thirsty, and cold. Your friends betrayed you. You lived a really hard life and even died so that I could know You. How amazing You are! You know everything about me, God. You see all the times I sin, yet still, You love me and want me to call You Father. You never leave me, and Your love is perfect. Thank You for loving us with an always and forever love.
We love You, God. Amen.

Joseph

READ MATTHEW 1:16-25

The last people in Jesus's family tree are his parents, Joseph and Mary. Mary and Joseph were engaged to be married. One day, Joseph's ordinary life was totally changed when an angel appeared to him in a dream. The angel said that Mary was pregnant with the baby that God had been promising all along. Joseph didn't know how Mary could be pregnant because they weren't married yet, but the angel told him that the Holy Spirit gave her the child. This baby was the One that God said would come from the line of David and would save God's people from their sins.

Joseph came from the family of David and probably grew up learning all about this promised child who would be born into his family. Can you imagine what it would be like to hear that the woman you were going to marry would carry the One you had grown up hearing all about? Not only that, but God also chose Joseph to be the father. The angel told him to name the baby Jesus because He would save God's people from their sins. The baby would be called Immanuel, which means "God is with us." Joseph had faith in God and obeyed Him.

Mary and Joseph got married and traveled to Bethlehem, and Mary gave birth to Jesus Christ, Immanuel. This baby is the answer to all of God's promises. He brought Jesus to the world through a line of ordinary and imperfect people. The birth of Jesus is very good news because, through Him, God made a way for us to be saved and be with Him forever.

DISCUSS TOGETHER

WHAT DO YOU THINK YOU WOULD HAVE DONE
WHEN THE ANGEL CAME IF YOU WERE JOSEPH?

GOD CALLED AN ORDINARY MAN LIKE JOSEPH TO BE
THE EARTHLY FATHER OF THE SAVIOR OF THE WORLD!
WHAT DOES THIS SAY ABOUT HOW GOD CAN USE OUR
ORDINARY LIVES FOR HIS BIG PURPOSES?

Prayer

Dear Lord, we praise You for Your extraordinary
plan of salvation. We praise You that You loved us
and desired a relationship with us to the extent that
You would make a way to send in Your one and only
Son to save us from our sin. We thank You for using
ordinary people like Joseph and like us to accomplish
Your great and glorious purposes. May we be faithful
and obedient to what You ask of us. Amen.

Draw a picture

about what you learned today.

Mary the Favored Woman

READ LUKE 1:26-56

Mary was an ordinary girl living in the town of Nazareth. Her family was poor and was ruled by King Herod, who was a wicked and cruel leader in the Roman government. Even through terrible times, God saw Mary and cared for her. Mary's life seemed unimportant, but God chose to use her for His great mission to save His people.

One day, God sent the angel, Gabriel, to visit Mary. Gabriel told her that she would give birth to Jesus, the Son of God. Jesus would be the true leader. He would be the promised King whose kingdom would never end. He would defeat all evil rulers and establish God's holy land. Mary did not know how this could happen since she was not married yet, but Gabriel told her about God's power. God miraculously gave a son to her cousin, Elizabeth, who couldn't have babies, so God would surely form a child inside Mary too. Mary believed in the promises of God. She knew the Lord promised to save people from sin and give hope and peace. Mary knew God was faithful, so she obeyed Him.

After an encouraging visit with Elizabeth, Mary recited a song of praise to God. She rejoiced in His holy name, love, and grace. Salvation was coming soon, and it was coming through her. Mary held Jesus who was both her son and the Son of God the Father. She waited for Jesus to come, looking forward to the day when He would be birthed into the world He would save.

WHY DO YOU THINK GOD CHOSE MARY TO BE
THE MOTHER OF JESUS?

WHY DID JESUS BECOME A PERSON?

Prayer

Dear Father, You see the lowly, and You care for the
poor in spirit. You are always near to Your people when
they are suffering. We thank You for Your steadfast love
that lasts throughout the generations. We are grateful
for Your commitment to Your word and Your working
in the life of Mary. We thank You for Jesus, who from
baby to adulthood, always lived a life pleasing to You.
We ask that when we remember baby Jesus, we think
about Your plan to save and the mission that was
accomplished. And, we ask that we have servant
hearts that seek Your glory. Amen.

Draw a picture

about what you learned today.

God Dwells With Us

READ MATTHEW 1:16, 18-25, EXODUS 29:45-46

Have you ever heard the word "Immanuel"? You might hear that word around Christmas time. But what exactly does it mean? And why was it a big deal that the prophet Isaiah said that there would be a baby born whose name would be called Immanuel? Immanuel means "God with us." Did you know that God has always wanted to be with His people? He created humans to be with Him. But then Adam and Eve sinned, and people could no longer have that close, face to face relationship with God. But even though they sinned, God still made a way to come close to His people

In the Old Testament, God's people built a tent for God to live in, called a tabernacle. A big cloud came down on the temple, and the presence of God went inside. But that was just not the same as the face to face relationship God once had with Adam and Eve. Later, He lived in a building called a temple. God was near His people, but His presence was separate from them. The story gets worse though. One day the people acted so sinfully for so long that God's presence left the temple. The people were left longing, hoping, and waiting. Surely the promise of Immanuel would still come.

And He did. When Jesus came as a baby, the presence of God came to us. All of the longing and waiting and hoping for a savior since the days of Adam and Eve was now fulfilled. God had come to live among His people. Can you imagine—God, whose glory filled the temple, now lay His head in Mary's arms? That is pretty incredible, right? But this was God's good plan to redeem the world and to once again be with His people.

READ JOHN 1:14. SPEND SOME TIME MAKING A LITTLE
SONG OR A RHYTHMIC CHANT WITH YOUR FAMILY.
RECITE THE VERSE TOGETHER.

WHY IS IT IMPORTANT THAT GOD BECAME MAN
AND WAS AMONG US?

Prayer

God, thank You for coming to us. Thank You that Jesus
is the fulfillment of the prophecy from Isaiah—that a
savior would come, and His name would be Immanuel.
It is hard for us to understand God coming as a man,
and much less, as a baby. But this is the beauty of God
being born in flesh. Jesus, You have become like us in
every way to save us in every way. We praise You, Jesus,
for that gospel truth. Help us not forget the beauty in
Your coming as a baby. May we rejoice that Immanuel
has come. In Jesus's name, Amen.

Draw a picture

about what you learned today.

Christ The Savior is Born

**READ MATTHEW 1:21, MARK 10:45,
LUKE 2:41-52, JOHN 1:29**

We usually finish the Christmas season thinking about Jesus's birth in Bethlehem, but that is not where the story ends. Did you know that Jesus was actually born to die? Jesus came to save His people from their sins, and He would do that by dying for them.

Jesus lived perfectly without sinning. He never complained or was selfish or mean. He taught people about God's kingdom, healed the sick, fed the hungry, rebuked the proud, raised the dead, and preached about salvation. He was fully God and fully man. He showed the world who God was and made a way for us to know God. The religious leaders of Jesus's day did not like Him or His message. They did not believe He was God's Son. The more Jesus preached about how He would save sinners, the angrier they became. Jesus knew that they planned to kill Him, but He also knew that God's plan to save sinners would be accomplished through His own death. He gave His life willingly for us (John 10:18).

During the Jewish celebration of Passover, Jesus was betrayed by one of His disciples and arrested by the religious leaders. He was mocked, stripped, beaten, and nailed to a cross outside the city of Jerusalem. He willingly gave up His life and carried the weight of God's righteous wrath for our sin upon His shoulders. He died in our place, paying the penalty of death for our sin (Romans 6:23).

But just like Jesus's story did not end in Bethlehem, His story did not end at the cross either. Three days later, God raised Him from the dead in victory over sin, Satan, and death. The resurrection assures us that when we believe in Jesus for salvation, we will be resurrected one day, too. We will enjoy life with Him forever in heaven where we will be free from sin, death, and sadness. When we celebrate the birth of Jesus each December, we are celebrating so much more than His birth. We are celebrating His life, death, and life again, for it is through His death and resurrection that we find forgiveness of sins and eternal life. He accomplished what He came to do. He saves His people from their sins!

DISCUSS TOGETHER

WHY DID JESUS COME TO US?
TRY TO RECITE MATTHEW 1:21 TOGETHER.

HAVE YOU BELIEVED IN JESUS'S SACRIFICE
FOR YOUR SINS? WHY OR WHY NOT?

Prayer

Dear God, thank You for sending Jesus to die for us in our place. We could not fix our own problem of sin, but You made a way for us to be forgiven and saved through Jesus's sacrifice on the cross. Help us to believe the good news about Jesus's death and resurrection and to share this message with our friends, family, and neighbors. Thank You for saving us from our sins! Amen.

Draw a pitcure

about what you learned today.

The Second Advent

READ JOHN 14:1-7, REVELATION 21:1-8

Today is the Day! Christmas is finally here! Today we celebrate that Jesus Christ was born for us. Christmas day will come and go, but the good news is that we have something else to look forward to. All the time we have spent waiting for Christmas helps us to wait for another wonderful day. On Christmas, we remember that Jesus came to the world, and one day, He is going to come back again. The day He returns will be a happier day than we could ever imagine.

Christmas is a time to celebrate, but it does not mean everything is perfect. Bad things and sad things still happen all the time, and we have God with us to help us through it all. But when Jesus comes back, all the bad and sad things will be over. We will not cry anymore. We will not get hurt anymore. We will not be sad or scared or lonely anymore. When Jesus comes again, He will make all things new, and it will be even better than Christmas day.

> ALL THE TIME WE HAVE SPENT WAITING FOR CHRISTMAS HELPS US TO WAIT FOR ANOTHER WONDERFUL DAY.

**DISCUSS
TOGETHER**

WHY ARE YOU HAPPY THAT JESUS
CAME TO THE WORLD?

WHY ARE YOU EXCITED FOR JESUS
TO COME AGAIN?

Prayer

Dear God, thank You for sending Jesus to the
world to die for our sins. Thank You for always
being with us. When things are hard or sad, help
us to remember that Jesus is going to come again
and make all things new. Amen.

Draw a picture
about what you learned today.

REFLECTION & FAMILY ACTIVITY

Create a Nativity Placemat

Throughout this study, we have learned about Jesus's family tree and all of the ordinary, broken people God used in His family line. This week, we focused on His earthly parents, Mary and Joseph, and we talked briefly about Jesus's birth in Bethlehem. But we were also reminded that His birth was not the end of the story. It was only the beginning. Jesus was the fulfillment of the promised Savior and King who gave his life on the cross to save us from our sin when we trust in Him.

As a reminder of Jesus's gift to us, each family member can make his or her own placemat to be used for the day. On a large sheet of construction paper, use the stencils of Mary, Joseph, baby Jesus, and the star of Bethlehem that are provided on pages 99–105 to cut out and trace or glue onto your piece of construction paper. You may choose instead to draw your own nativity using crayons or markers and even add a stable and animals. Once you have finished the nativity scene of Jesus's family, use contact paper to cover both sides of your placemat to protect it from any spills. Once Christmas is over, tuck them away to pull back out to use and enjoy again next Christmas!

Mary

Joseph

Baby Jesus

Star of Bethlehem

Thank you for studying
God's Word with us!

CONNECT WITH US

@thedailygraceco

@kristinschmucker

CONTACT US

info@thedailygraceco.com

SHARE

#thedailygraceco

#lampandlight

VISIT US ONLINE

thedailygraceco.com

MORE DAILY GRACE

The Daily Grace App

Daily Grace Podcast